TRUCKS

Katie Daynes

Designed by Zöe Wray

Illustrations by Christyan Fox

Truck consultant: David Riley

Reading consultant: Alison Kelly, Roehampton University

Contents

Truck travel

Trucks carry all kinds of things from one place to another.

The things a truck carries are called its load.

Trucks and trailers

Some trucks come in two parts. The trailer is where the load is kept and the cab is where the driver sits.

Trailer

Cab

Wires and tubes carry electricity and air to the trailer. These make the back lights and brakes work.

The trailer
rests on two
landing legs.

The cab backs
up to meet
the trailer.

They join
together and
drive away.

When trailer trucks
reach a bend, the cab
turns first, then the trailer follows.

A cab can join up with
different shapes of trailers.

Truck bodies

Not all trucks have two parts. On many trucks the trailer is attached to the cab.

This truck is taking fresh bananas to a market

Some very small trucks only have three wheels.

Box body trucks have hard sides and open up at the back.

Soft-sided trucks have sides that open like a big curtain.

On flatbed trucks, the load lies flat on the trailer and is tied down with rope.

7

Loading up

Lots of trucks collect their loads from huge buildings called warehouses.

A forklift truck picks up a crate on a pallet.

It takes it outside and lifts it up onto a truck.

The crates are stacked inside the truck.

Some loads, such as racehorses, can walk onto their trucks.

This truck has its own crane. The driver is using it to load up.

On the road

Often trucks have to take their load somewhere far away.

The journey may take several days.

Many countries make drivers take a break during the day so they don't get too tired.

4:30

Truck drivers take breaks at truck stops.

On long journeys they can rest, eat and sleep in their trucks.

Inside the cab there is room to relax.

A bed folds down from the wall.

Across the sea

Trucks may have to take their loads across the sea on a ferry.

Trucks arrive at a port. They drive up a ramp, onto a ferry.

The ferry closes its back door and sets sail across the sea.

When it reaches land, the front of the ferry opens and the trucks drive off.

Some loads are lifted onto a ship, leaving the truck behind.

The ship crosses the sea and the load is put on another truck.

The load travels inside a box called a container. Cranes lift the containers on and off the ship.

Container crane

Containers

Tanker trucks

Tanker trucks carry liquids or gases in big tanks on their trailers.

Milk tankers collect milk from farms. The milk goes through a pipe into the tank.

Cows are milked twice a day. The tanker collects the milk on the same day.

Fuel tankers take
fuel to gas stations.

At the gas station,
pipes are attached
to the tanker.

The fuel goes from
the tanker into big
tanks under the ground.

Fuel
tank

Fuel
tank

Dump trucks

Dump trucks are huge trucks that carry sand, dirt and chunks of rock.

The driver has to climb up some steps to reach the cab.

A big digger fills the truck with scoops of dirt.

The truck takes the dirt away, then dumps it out.

Some dump trucks have wheels taller than two tall men.

Fire trucks

Fire trucks bring firefighters, ladders and water to places where there's a fire.

The firefighters open up the side to reach their equipment.

They unwind hoses and attach them to the truck's water tank.

If the water tank runs out, they use water from pipes under the ground.

Ladders stretch up from the back of the trucks and firefighters spray water on the fire.

Some fire trucks have platforms that reach up to rescue people.

Heavy loads

Trucks that carry big, heavy loads have many wheels or move on tracks.

This transporter truck is carrying a space shuttle. Can you see the truck cab?

The transporter takes the shuttle into a warehouse.

Cranes help lift the shuttle onto a crawler truck.

Space shuttle

The crawler has
tracks instead
of wheels.
It carries the
shuttle to its
launch pad.

Track

The shuttle crawler travels even slower than
a person walking.

Dirty work

Trashmen collect trash and carry it away in trash trucks.

A dumpster is hooked onto the truck. It is lifted up and the trash is tipped out.

A big metal plate squashes down the trash to make more room.

To empty the truck, the end lifts up and a metal plate pushes the trash out.

A bigger truck takes the trash to a place where it can be burned or buried.

Some trash can be used again. This dump truck is delivering plastic bags to a recycling plant.

Hot and cold

Around the world, trucks are shaped differently to suit the jobs they do.

Road trains are big trucks with several trailers

They travel long distances on very straight roads. Some drive all the way across deserts.

Road trains meet very little traffic so they can travel quickly.

In snowy mountains,
trucks are used to flatten
the snow on the ski slopes.

They have tracks instead of wheels to keep
them from slipping on the snow.

The front of the
truck scoops snow
out of the way.

At the back there
are brushes to
smooth the snow.

Car transporters

Car transporters carry cars to garages.
Follow the numbers to see how they load up

Deck

1. A car reverses onto a deck and is tipped up.

2. Two cars follow, then that deck is raised.

Some trucks have more than 50 wheels.

3. Three cars drive onto a deck above the cab.

4. Six more cars fit onto other decks below.

Truck sports

Some trucks don't carry loads. Instead they take part in truck sports.

These trucks are having a race. They drive around a track at high speeds.

Some very fast trucks have jet engines, just like planes.

Once a year there is a truck race that goes across the Sahara desert and takes 21 days.

Monster trucks take part in jumping competitions.

| The monster truck speeds up a ramp. | It jumps up and over a big object. | Then it lands with a bump on the ground. |

Glossary of truck words

Here are some of the words in this book you might not know. This page tells you what they mean.

 load - the things carried by a truck.

 cab - the front part of a truck where the truck driver sits.

 trailer - a load carrier on wheels that is pulled by a truck.

 pallet - a big tray used in warehouses. Forklift trucks lift up crates on pallets.

 truck stop - like a parking lot, but for trucks. Drivers can stay the night here.

 ferry - a boat that takes people, trucks and cars across the sea.

 recycling - making new objects from old objects that are collected by trucks.

Websites to visit

If you have a computer, you can find out more about trucks on the Internet. On the Usborne Quicklinks Website there are links to four fun websites.

Website 1 - Make different trucks with the three cards on your screen.

Website 2 - Find out more about dump trucks and building sites.

Website 3 - See photos of trucks from around the world.

Website 4 - Learn what each part of a fire truck does.

To visit these websites, go to **www.usborne-quicklinks.com** Read the Internet safety guidelines, and then type the keywords "beginners trucks".

The websites are regularly reviewed and the links in Usborne Quicklinks are updated. However, Usborne Publishing is not responsible, and does not accept liability, for the content or availability of any website other than its own. We recommend that children are supervised while on the Internet.

Index

Acknowledgements

Photographic manipulation by Emma Julings and John Russell.
American editor Carrie Armstrong

Photo credits
The publishers are grateful to the following for permission to reproduce material:
© **Alvey & Towers** Cover, 1, 5, 28, © **Bill Noonan, Boston Fire Department** 19,
© **Corbis** (Kevin R. Morris) 6, (Joseph Sohm; ChromoSohm Inc.) 9, (Ted Spiegel) 11,
(Richard Hamilton Smith) 16-17, (Richard T. Nowitz) 23, (Christine Osborne) 24,
© **The Dairy Council** 14, © **Digital Vision** 4, 10, 12-13, 16-17, 23, 24, © **ECM (Vehicle
Delivery Service) Ltd** 26-27, © **Kässbohrer Geländefahrzeug AG (PistenBully)** 25,
© **Malcolm Birks** 31, © **NASA** 20, 21, © **Nissan/dppi** 29, © **Volvo Truck Limited** 2-3, 15

With thanks to
Henry Brook, Chris Hodge Trucks (www.chrishodgetrucks.co.uk),
Bill Noonan, Steven Askew, Wolfgang Lutz and The Dairy Council

Sun, Moon and Stars

Farm animals

Elizabeth I

TRASH AND RECYCLING

Dogs

Horses and ponies

Spiders

Planes

Ancient Greeks

Cats

VOLCANOES

DINOSAURS

Your Body

Armor

Sharks

Celts

Vikings

Castles

How flowers grow

Knights

Living in space

Caterpillars and Butterflies

Ballet

Pirates

Egyptians

Eggs and Chicks

Romans

Weather

Tadpoles and frogs

Why do we eat?

Under the sea

Bears